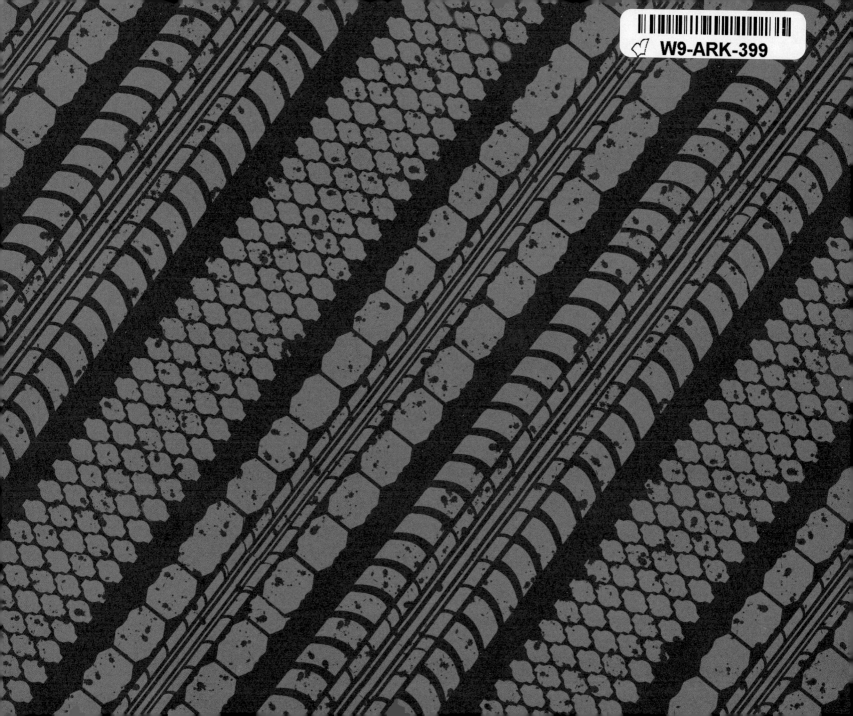

GREAT

MONSTER TRUCKS

GREAT
MONSTER TRUCKS

A STUNNING COLLECTION OF THESE GIANT MACHINES

PaRragon

Bath · New York · Singapore · Hong Kong · Cologne · Delhi
Melbourne · Amsterdam · Johannesburg · Auckland · Shenzhen

First published by Parragon in 2011

Parragon
Queen Street House
4 Queen Street
Bath BA1 1HE, UK

Designed, produced, and packaged by
Stonecastle Graphics Limited

Designed by Paul Turner and Sue Pressley
Text by Lisa Morris
Edited by Philip de Ste. Croix

ISBN 978-1-4454-2890-1

Printed in China

Page 1: *Dirt Devil.*

Page 2: *Swamp Thing.*

Page 3: *Red Dragon and Bigfoot®.*

Right: *High Maintenance.*

Contents

Introduction

The world of monster trucks sprang into life in 1975 when a businessman named Bob Chandler started to make his standard pickup truck bigger and bigger by putting on ever-larger tires to publicize his four-wheel-drive business. In 1981 he drove the truck, now known as Bigfoot®, over a number of old cars in a field—a feat he repeated a few months later in a stadium in front of an audience. The rest, as they say, is history! Now, some 35 years later, monster trucks have evolved to become a truly global multimillion-dollar industry.

In the United States monster truck displays regularly fill stadiums packed with up to 70,000 fans, who thrill to watch car-crushing freestyle or head-to-head racing. Most monster truck teams have merchandise for sale at the shows and also via their own websites, and the Internet age has seen the rise of web forums where monster truck fans can share their enthusiasm and exchange information online.

These powerful machines run on racing methanol that is forced into the big engines by superchargers and fuel injection, delivering performance of up to 2,000 bhp. Their enormous tires, measuring 66 in x 43 in x 25 in (1.7 m x 1.1 m x 0.6 m), give the trucks their characteristic appearance and they weigh in at about half a ton each.

The world of monster trucks is a distinctly colorful one! From darkest black through vibrant oranges, pinks, and purples, the bodywork of these magnificent machines reflects the personalities and interests of their owners. To watch a machine that weighs approximately 5 tons fly effortlessly over cars at high speed is an experience never to be forgotten. Once you have seen these magnificent beasts spinning into a "donut" and disappearing in a cloud of dust, or traveling fast on just their two rear wheels, you will forever be a monster truck fan.

Right: Samson's unique bodywork makes it a widely recognized truck—its painted muscular arms represent the strength of Samson. Seen here racing head-to-head against Full Boar, both drivers are going all out to win, although Samson is leading by a full truck length.

Beauty and the Beasts

Below: *Thrasher is unique among monster trucks touring the American circuit in that it is based on a Japanese Toyota Tundra pickup truck and not the more usual American truck bodies made by Ford, Chevrolet, and Dodge. With its custom-built shocks, Thrasher stands 10 ft 6 in (3.2 m) tall.*

Opposite: *Bigfoot® 17 is the only official Bigfoot® monster truck to be located outside of the United States. It was built in 2003 in the United Kingdom and is owned and operated by Nigel and Lisa Morris. It features a 572 ci (9.4 liter) Ford supercharged V8, which runs on methanol.*

Below: *Grave Digger was originally built by Dennis Anderson from North Carolina. This truck is famous for its "no fear" approach to racing and impressive freestyle performances, often being prepared to go the extra mile to please its fans.*

Opposite: *What instantly makes Monster Patrol stand out is the huge customized aerodynamic wing fitted to the rear of this 2002 Chevrolet-based truck. Hailing from Indiana, owner Paul Shafer has been racing monster trucks since 1993.*

Opposite: Originally driven by Jeff Perrin, and now by his wife Jocelyn, High Maintenance is a family-run truck whose body style is derived from a 1940 Willy's pickup truck.

Left: Avid outdoors man Scott Hartsock retired after 15 years as a gunsmith to become a monster truck owner and driver. His background in weaponry inspired the name Gun Slinger.

Below: Podzilla is based on a Chevy K1500 truck with a blown and injected engine, which produces some 1,350 bhp to propel the 5-ton monster from 0 to 60 mph (97 kph) in six seconds.

Right: In 2004 owner and driver Chris Bergeron decided to build a concept body resembling a dog for his Brutus truck. It was based on sketches by artist Jason Becker.

Opposite: Red Dragon takes it name from the Welsh national symbol and is driven by Rob Williams. Built in 2004, this was the second tube-framed monster truck to be built in Wales.

Below: Continuing the animal theme, Spike Unleashed was custom built by Avenger Racing. It features a 3D Siberian husky concept body design by Jason Becker.

Far left: Located in Tuscon, Arizona, Nasty Boy features a 1940 Willy's truck body with a 468 ci (7.7 liter) Chevy V8 producing around 1,200 bhp. It is operated by Sturges Motorsports.

Left: Originally driven by Sam Sturges of Tucson, Arizona, Unnamed & Untamed features a 1942 Dodge panel wagon body. It has been driven by his nephew Travis since 1997.

Below: Built in 1996 as a Chevrolet S10, Jim Koehler's Avenger is a favorite with fans. In 2002 Jim turned the truck world on its head by debuting a 1957 Chevy Belair car body on Avenger.

Right: In 2003 lighting designer Jay Snyder and some friends bought Screamin' Demon and rebuilt the chassis, moving the left-drive steering to center-drive and remounting the engine.

Far right: Number 2 truck in the Hall Brothers Racing Inc. Team, Rammunition is driven by Geremie Dishman, who won the 2006 Dodge Monster Truck Thunder Drags Series.

Below: Rich Blackburne is a true privateer in every sense of the word. Rich has a full-time job, but runs his truck Viper at as many shows as his busy schedule allows.

Opposite: With a chassis built by Tim Barks, Thunderbolt made its debut at the 2009 Truckfest event in Peterborough, England.

Above: Karl Swallow's entire family have been involved in the building and running of Slingshot—definitely a family affair!

Right: Bad News Racing works primarily with the Monster Jam Tour in their Thunder Nationals and Summer Heat Series.

Far right: An 530 ci (8.7 liter) Dart engine, fitted to a race source chassis, powers the 2002 Chevrolet 2500 HD-bodied The Patriot.

Far left: *Firestarter is a one-third-scale monster truck from Ontario, Canada. It is based on actual firefighting pumpers from the 1930s and has a dual chain drive.*

Left: *With years of experience as an engineer, Jimmy Creten's greatest feat so far has to be winning the 2005 Monster Jam Freestyle Championships in The Bounty Hunter.*

Below: *Sudden Impact Racing Team owner Brandon Legarde is a true innovator, developing his own unique version of monster truck tires, namely the SIR monster truck racing tire.*

Left: *The Broker was a privateer monster truck that raced in the USHRA Monster Jam series. It began life as the Thrasher and then the chassis was sold to Jim Leahy in 2002, when he rebuilt the truck from the ground up and renamed it.*

Opposite: *A very recognizable monster truck in the United States, Madusa is driven by world wrestling champion Debra Miceli (ring name Madusa), who has won the women's WWF title in World Championship Wrestling on three occasions. In 1999 Madusa entered the world of monster trucks by competing in the Monster Jam series.*

Right: The prehistoric-looking Jurassic Attack was based on the head of a triceratops dinosaur—3D body monster trucks have become very popular over the years.

Far right: From Chicago, Illinois, Monster Mutt is a definite kids' favorite with its floppy ears and pink tongue. A 1951 Mercury body styled as a Dalmatian dog is the latest version.

Below: Monster trucks come in all shapes and styles and it is not uncommon to see such wild combinations as a dinosaur concept competing against a martial arts theme.

Left and below: *The craze for modifying pickup trucks sprang up in the United States in the late 1970s as competitions for truck-pulling began to take off. Owners began making their trucks increasingly tall to compete in "mud-bogging" events. Since the first days of monster trucks, these powerful machines have entertained the public by crushing cars using their brute power, and this is now a popular part of displays. Despite being huge, monster trucks have a low center of gravity and four-wheel drive, which increases their stability and enables them to navigate tricky and uneven terrain and to maneuver over the bodies of the smaller cars they are demolishing.*

Right: *As the name suggests, Backwards Bob is all about being backwards! The body is mounted back-to-front on the chassis.*

Far right: *Clearly modeled on an American fire-engine design, it is easy to see how Backdraft got its name.*

Opposite: *General Tire was made for four-wheel Jamborees. It nearly won the 2009 Monster Truck Thunder Drags.*

Below: *Based on a 2006 Dodge Ram and costing in excess of $150,000, monster trucks like Raminator do not come cheap!*

Monsters on Display

Right: One of the first trucks named after an advertisement, Minimizer has been driven since day one by Marc McDonald who was voted Monster Jam "Rookie of the Year" in 2006.

Below: Rap Attack monster truck, owned and driven by David Rappach, has its name emblazoned in lettering across the side panel and a distinctive neon-green chassis frame, which helps to keep the gigantic wheels in place.

Opposite: Monster trucks were originally slow, lumbering beasts barely able to climb over cars. During their 35-year history, they have evolved into purpose-built racing machines that literally fly over cars during head-to-head races. In today's monster truck events, which feature two trucks racing side by side, the results are often determined by a time interval as small as one-tenth of a second. Such fierce competition forces teams and drivers to strive continually to improve every aspect of their trucks' performance, be it engine power or the action of the suspension units. Every detail is analyzed with a view to improving results.

Below: Like most American motor sports, fans' loyalties are divided between the big three brands—Ford, Dodge, and Chevrolet. Tom Schmidt's 2001 Ford-bodied truck powered by a 460 Ford engine indicates that he is clearly a Ford man.

Opposite: Created in 2000 on a Dan Patrick chassis, Pure Adrenaline was driven for three years by Randy Brown. In the fall of 2002 he was asked to join the Grave Digger Fleet, making his debut in January 2003.

Left: *Monster truck originators Bigfoot® now have a truck permanently based in Europe. Here European Bigfoot® 17 is shown freestyling with sister truck Monstrous, which was built in 2005 by Bigfoot® 17 owner Nigel Morris.*

Below: *Car-crushing displays are currently one of the most popular monster truck events. Typically the truck would jump over six cars, but here Red Dragon leans dangerously to the left as this jump starts to go wrong.*

Right and opposite: Indoor-arena monster truck shows thrill crowds the world over. At these events you can watch these huge machines racing over cars, or freestyling—where the driver gets the chance to display his own driving style over a set time—and to show off with "sky wheelies" and "donuts."

Below: Former sharpshooter and expert gunsmith Scott Hartsock long had a dream to enter the world of monster trucks. He did just that in 1992, and now regularly competes with his truck Gun Slinger. He is also the proud owner of a second truck named Cowboy.

Opposite: Nicknamed "Air Man Dan," The Destroyer's driver Dan Evans is probably best known for his reverse jumps. In 2005 he jumped his truck over a bus stack and then a semi-trailer in reverse. In 2007 Dan ripped out the truck's right rear spindle bolts leaping over a double bus stack in reverse.

Left and below: Blue Thunder is sponsored by the Ford Motor Company truck division and is built both for promotional use and competition. Wanting a truck to portray its "Built Ford Tough" campaign, the body style is based on the F-series Ford pickup—like other trucks it is licensed for toys and video games.

Opposite: Vibrant paint schemes on monster trucks are an integral part of any show. Here thousands of fans are enjoying the performance while watching the brightly colored Red Dragon during a Monster Mania event in Estonia.

Below: The flight of a monster truck is rarely straight and true. Difficult landings are commonplace and often result in broken axle parts. Landing on one wheel, as Swamp Thing is about to do, is not a desirable option, though it often happens.

Opposite: The patented muscular arms that adorn Samson's flanks have made it one of the most iconic 3D character trucks.

Right: The first woman ever to win the Monster Jam World Finals, Madusa beat her trainer Dennis Anderson in the last race.

Far right: Superman uses the 540 Merlin engine to fly across the cars with ease, its cape appearing to float behind.

Below: When trucks go vertical, fans get a clear view of the ultra strong chassis, axles, and shock absorbers underneath.

Below: *This wonderfully charismatic truck is a definite hit with the fans. At 12 ft (3.6 m) wide and 10 ft (3 m) tall, the dog-shaped Brutus debuted in 2004. Operated by Team Scream, its pack members are Avenger and Spike, another 3D character truck.*

Opposite: *Team mate of Brutus and Avenger, Spike Unleashed takes its name from its collar. It was modeled on a Siberian husky featuring the characteristic black and white fur and blue eyes. The truck was built by Chris Bergeron.*

This page: Monster truck shows across the world feature many different trucks, some of them privately owned and some representing large corporate organizations. The one thing that unites them all is the high-action, adrenaline-filled, car-crushing spectacle. Some fans prefer the competitive thrill of side-by-side racing, while others revel in the freestyle displays where drivers exhibit their personal driving styles. In freestyle the trucks can be seen performing certain "standard" maneuvers that include "sky wheelie," "donut," "cyclone," and "long jump." Each driver will add their own individual variations to make their performance unique and memorable.

Far left: Gary Porter started competing in the Carolina Crusher in 1987 after setting up Porters 4x4 shop in 1981 with his brother. In 1992 the brothers built another truck, and in order to compete in three different monster truck series a third Carolina Crusher appeared for the 1994 season.

Left and below: Damon Bradshaw grew up competing in motocross, arenacross, and finally supercross events. Looking for a new challenge, he turned to the world of monster trucks and landed the job of driver for the US Air Force-sponsored Afterburner truck, which is painted air force blue and silver.

Below and opposite: Evidence that the popularity of monster trucks is truly global can be found in Hungary, where a group of pioneers have been working hard to build monster trucks from available parts. Though not "true" monster trucks as they lack the 66 in x 43 in x 25 in (1.7 m x 1.1 m x 0.6 m) tires required for a real monster, they are nevertheless impressive in their own right. These trucks share the bright paint schemes and striking body styles of their inspirational American big brothers.

Opposite: Nasty Boy provides a good view of the eight-point roll cage that sits under the bodywork of these trucks.

Right: Jimmy Creten in Bounty Hunter not only battles other trucks, but also his wife Dawn who drives Scarlet Bandit.

Far right: Many competitors use hand-cut monster truck tires, which help these huge machines gain extra traction.

Below: With a body that is officially classified as a "futuristic SUV," Maximum Destruction is instantly recognizable.

Opposite: Bigfoot® 4x4 Inc. were the original creators of US monster trucks. The UK's Bigfoot® 17 is here wearing its 30th Anniversary body, painted in 2005 to commemorate the firm's 30 years in the monster truck industry.

Below: Dirt Devil is a German-based monster truck operating in Europe. Here it is seen crushing a car at a small event. Car crushing has been popular since the earliest days of monster trucks and remains a firm favorite with fans around the world.

Above: *Heading over the cars with an initial "sky wheelie" gives the audience a fantastic view of the underside of these huge machines that they would otherwise rarely see.*

Left: *Here we see female monster truck driver Jocelyn Perrin at her finest, performing a perfect "sky wheelie" as High Maintenance comes into initial contact with the cars.*

Opposite: *Even in relatively small arenas these machines are still capable of putting on an amazing display, as exemplified here by Slingshot's huge signature jump across the cars.*

Above: *Iron Outlaw takes its name from a Wild West theme just like its stable partners, Bounty Hunter and Scarlet Bandit. All three trucks are owned by Kansas-based 2Xtreme Racing.*

Right: *Shod with its custom-cut tires, The Patriot was launched in June 2004 by Danny Rodoni who first came across monster trucks when helping Team Meents crew in his spare time.*

Below: *Created and situated in one of the world's most exotic locations, this truck is based at, and named after, Maui Off Road Center, Hawaii.*

Far left: Scarlet Bandit is driven by Jimmy Creten's wife Dawn, part of another family-run monster truck business. Competing since 1997, this former army medic and mother of three took home the 2004 "Crash Madness Award" from the USHRA for her dramatic front flip at the season's first event in Houston, Texas.

Left: While working in the St. Louis area of Missouri as an electrical contractor, former mud racer Doug Noelke decided that when he made the move to compete in monster trucks he needed to bring the name of his famous mud racer with him, and so the Big Dawg was born.

Above: Gun Slinger is coming in to land during a racing event where the lanes are often marked out using hay bales or brightly colored blocks known as tuff blocks. In most racing events a truck deviating from the demarcated course is either excluded from the race or receives a time penalty.

Left: Scott May's Daredevil Stunt Show offers British fans a fast moving, action-packed display of monster truck destruction. Built by Gary Porter in the United States and driven by him for some years as the Carolina Crusher, this truck was renamed Bandit and now resides permanently in the United Kingdom.

Thrills and Spills

Below: *When these huge beasts come under enormous pressures, breakages and mayhem often ensue. Here Monstrous makes a very hard landing, smashing off both front wheels and sliding along briefly on its front axle.*

Opposite: *In the heat of competition trucks and drivers are pushed to their limit. As Bigfoot ®17 flies across the final set of cars, its front right wheel is knocked off, narrowly missing the fiberglass body shell.*

Opposite: Rollovers and crashes are quite a common sight at monster truck events due to the extreme nature of the courses and obstacles. These can include stacks of cars, pickups, motor homes, buses, garbage trucks, and even boats.

Below: Even though Monster Mutt, like all monster trucks, is equipped with front and rear steering that can operate independently of each other, sometimes even this amount of control is not enough to save the truck from a rollover.

Opposite and left: It takes more than a rollover and a bit of damaged bodywork to stop driver Dennis Anderson and his iconic truck Grave Digger. Dennis has built his reputation on his fearless freestyle runs, but he let his emotions show in 2004 when he won the Monster Jam Racing World Finals.

Below: Known to his many fans as "Mr. Entertainment," Avenger driver Jim Koehler will stop at nothing to please his audience. As well as jumping his truck over pretty much anything that he finds in his path, Jim has even been known to jump into the water feature at the Las Vegas World Finals.

Below: The "donut" or "cyclone" has to be the ultimate spectacle for fans. It always provokes huge cheers and excited applause from the audience as they watch a monster truck spin in a tight circle throwing up clouds of dust and dirt.

Opposite: Disappearing behind a thick cloud of dust and smoke Bigfoot®17 makes this feat look so easy! With one or more wheels lifting off the ground as it rotates at high speed, this is definitely a heart-stopping moment for the driver!

Above: *Sometimes when these machines land over a stack of cars at full power, the truck will bounce back up from the landing causing a "slap wheelie."*

Left: *Three times Guinness World Record holder Bigfoot®16 driver Dan Runte performs his signature power wheelie as the bar drags along the ground spraying sparks in its wake.*

Right: *When the stresses and strains of competition prove just too much for these mighty machines, they end up being towed back to the pits for some well-deserved TLC!*

Index

Picture credits
a = above, b = below, l = left, r = right,
c = center

© shutterstock.com: Peter Albrektsen
11; Walter G Arce 28, 29, 43al, 47ac;
Julian Camilo Bernal 19br; Christopher
Halloran 16al, 16ac, 16b, 46, 47ar;
Marcel Janocovic 1, 49; JustASC 10;
Nagy Melinda 44, 45; Alex Melnick 47b;
Felix Mizioznikov 13a, 32a, 32b, 34, 35a,
35b, 56, 57, 58, 59l; Raigl 22b; Barry
Salmons 6–7, 26a, 26b, 27, 33; Melvin
Schlubman 20cr; Maksim Shmeljov 2,
9, 36, 37; Michael Stokes 3, 15, 48.

© Creative Commons License:
battlecreek 17ar; Lance Cheung 43ac;
DanDeChiaro 38; mandolin davis 52bl;
Divik 24ar, 42al, 42ar; jurvetson 52r;
Kildare2 20al; Mypoorbrain 22ar, 24ac,
42ac, 42cl; Jot Powers 19bc, 20ac, 52al,
53al, 53ac, 53cr; Tammy Powers 22ac;
Senior Airman Larry E. Reid Jnr 43b;
Termin8ter 59r; thomascrenshaw 8,
17ac, 17b, 20bl, 21, 39ac, 39ar, 39b,
42br; Luc Viatour 23a, 23b; www.
theedinburghblog.co.uk 53bl.

© MonsterPhotos/Lisa Ames: 4–5, 12,
13b, 14a, 14b, 18, 19a, 24b, 25, 30–31,
32, 40, 41, 50, 51l, 51r, 54, 55, 60, 61,
62l, 62r, 63.

The author and publishers have made
every reasonable effort to credit
all copyright holders. Any errors or
omissions that may have occurred are
inadvertent and anyone who for any
reason has not been credited is invited
to write to the publishers so that a full
acknowledgment may be made in
subsequent editions of this work.

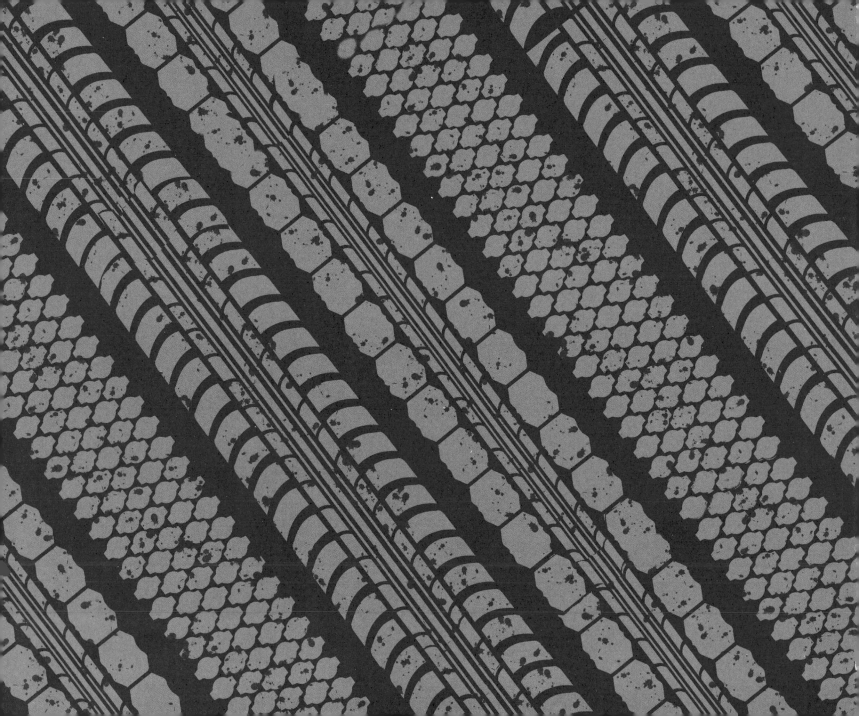